The Voices of ALOHA

DAUGHTERS OF THE KING, VOL 1
A CHOIR OF HOPE

FEATURING

Michelle A. G. Ebalaroza Kawano

Amy Colter

Jennifer Kotel

Felicia S. Collins

Bri-Anne Banglos

Emari Hunn

Mary Huhnholz

Voices of ALOHA: Daughters of the King VOL 1

A Choir of Hope

This book is a work of collaborative testimony. The stories contained herein are shared with permission by the contributors and reflect their personal experiences, faith journeys, and perspectives. Names, identifying details, and circumstances may have been changed to protect privacy where requested.

This book is not intended to replace professional medical, psychological, legal, or pastoral counseling. Readers are encouraged to seek qualified support for matters related to mental health, trauma recovery, abuse, addiction, or other sensitive concerns. Reading discretion is advised.

Scripture quotations are taken from the Holy Bible, New Living Translation (NLT), unless otherwise noted. Used by permission. All rights reserved.

Because of the dynamic nature of the Internet, any web address or links contained in this book may have changed since publication and may no longer be valid. The views expressed in this work are solely those of the author's and do not necessarily reflect the views of the publisher, and the publisher disclaims any responsibility for them

Editor & Visionary:
Michelle A. G. Ebalaroza Kawano
Printed in the United States of America

ISBN:
E Book: 979-8-9911622-2-7
Paperback: 979-8-9911622-3-4

VOICES OF ALOHA; DAUGHTERS OF THE KING VOL. 1

A Choir of Hope

Blessed To Be A Blessing Worldwide Publishing ©2026

TABLE OF CONTENTS

ACKNOWLEDGEMENTS & THANKS

First and always, to God, The Great I Am ~

My Creator, my Sustainer, and the Author of every story represented in these pages. Thank You for the calling, the obedience, the creativity, and the grace to steward voices that matter. Thank You for reminding me that this work was never meant to be done alone, and that when You ask for a choir, You provide the voices. All glory, honor, and praise belong to You.

To my husband, Bruce ~

Thank you for your patience, your encouragement, and your unwavering support through the late nights, early mornings, and long hours spent in the studio. Thank you for putting up with my creative chaos, for believing in the vision even when it required sacrifice, and for loving me so faithfully as I followed God's call. I could not do this without you, nor would I want to.

To the courageous women who lent their voices to this beautifully powerful anthology ~

Amy Colter, Jennifer Kotel, Felicia S. Collins, Bri-Anne Banglos, Emari Hunn, and Mary Huhnholz; thank you for trusting me with your stories. Thank you for your honesty, your vulnerability, and your willingness to share what was sacred, difficult, and deeply personal. Your voices form this Choir of Hope, and each testimony carries healing not only for the reader, but for generations to come.

To every voice who continues the Voices of ALOHA ~

Those who are reading these pages and feel the stirring to share your own stories; thank you in advance for your courage. This movement continues because voices rise, stories are told, and faith overcomes fear. Your bravery breaks the silence and continues the song. There is room in this choir for you.

To every reader who opened this book ~

Thank you for listening. Thank you for honoring these stories with care and compassion. May what you read here remind you that you are seen, deeply loved, and never alone.

With gratitude, faith, and aloha,

Michelle A. G. Ebalaroza Kawano aka *MAGEK*
Founder, Voices of ALOHA
Blessed To Be A Blessing Worldwide Publishing
MAGEK.Blessings@gmail.com

Ladies, bringing you all together has been such a blessing to me. As I carefully and gently read through each of your stories, I couldn't help but ache for the pain you endured in your past; but I celebrate who you are today. Your courage is not just in what you survived, but in what you chose to share.

Thank you for lending your voice. Thank you for speaking up for those who sat silent for too long. You have given permission to the one who thought she had to stay quiet. You have given action to the one who kept saying, "Maybe next time." You have given faith to the one who questioned and doubted herself.

I want to be the first to say thank you. As the pebble takes that first splash in the water and the ripples move outward, there will be many more thank yous that follow; echoes of gratitude from lives

● ● ●

you may never meet but deeply impact through your generous vulnerability.

I love you, Sisters. This is only the beginning. May the Voices of ALOHA continue to rise through the ages.

A Hui Hou. ~ MAGEK

Chapter One

A CHOIR OF HOPE

by: Michelle A. G. Ebalaroza Kawano

There are moments in life when a single voice is not enough.

Moments when pain is too heavy, silence too loud, and healing too fragile to be carried alone. In those moments, God does something extraordinary—He gathers voices. Not identical voices. Not perfected ones. But willing voices. Broken voices. Brave voices. Voices that have lived through the night and still choose to sing at dawn.

That is what you are holding in your hands.

This book is not a collection of stories by chance. It is a choir—a sacred gathering of women who have walked through fire, loss, betrayal, fear, trauma, and doubt, and who are still standing. Each woman sings her own note. Each testimony carries its own tone, tempo, and texture. And together, they form a harmony called *hope*.

• • •

A choir does not require every singer to sound the same. In fact, its beauty comes from difference—soprano and alto, strength and softness, trembling beginnings and confident declarations. Some voices rise boldly. Others quiver as they whisper truth for the first time. Yet every voice matters. Every voice belongs.

So before you read another page, let this be your invitation:

You do not need to rush.
You do not need to compare.
You do not need to be "strong" while reading these pages.

You only need to listen.

How This Choir Was Born

Before this book became a collection of voices, it began as a promise.

In 2023, when I wrote my first book, *Walking in ALOHA: 5 Steps to Living My God Potential Life,* I made a commitment to the Lord. I promised Him that every year I would publish a written work—not for recognition, not for numbers, but as an act of

● ● ●

obedience and worship. I wanted to honor Him as my Creator by allowing His creativity to flow through me, year after year.

And so, it was.

In 2024, I published again. *31 Steps to Mastery: Essential Toolkits for Personal and Professional Success* became my first self-published book—a milestone that stretched my faith, my discipline, and my confidence.

Then came 2025.

I sat down to write as I always had, expecting the words to come. I knew the title. It rang loud and clear in my spirit: *Voices of ALOHA*. But this time, the words were hard to put down. I struggled. I prayed. I questioned why something that felt so right was suddenly so difficult.

One day, in prayer, I asked the Lord why the resistance felt so strong.

As I repeated the word aloud—*Voices… Voices…* the answer came with clarity and conviction:

"Voices."

Not voice.

Voices.

"I need a choir for this one." I heard the Lord say.

Tears filled my eyes then, and they still do now, because at that moment I realized how close I had come to missing something sacred. I had been focused on *my* assignment, *my* publishing goal, *my* promise to produce something.

But God wasn't asking me to write alone.

He was asking me to gather.

That was the moment the *Voices of ALOHA* movement was born.

I began reaching out; having conversations, sending messages, asking questions that felt both simple and holy: *Would you like to share your story? Would you like to give your testimony a voice? Would you like to become a published author?*

There was no contract. No financial incentive. No guarantee— except this: that their stories would be honored, preserved, and given life and legacy.

What these women offered was priceless. And what God formed through their willingness was far greater than anything I could have written alone.

This book exists because obedience shifted from "me" to "we."

And when voices come together in surrender, God creates harmony.

Then the unexpected happened.

In the midst of this unfolding journey, my pastor called me and asked if I would participate in a book project with our church. The invitation was simple and humbling: I would write one chapter, and several other members of the church would write chapters as well. Our names would not appear in the book. There would be no individual recognition—only obedience and service.

I said yes.

God blessed me with the honor of writing the very first chapter, and on October 14, 2025, the book was published, *Reach People: Multiplication Through Discipleship* by Inspire Church. In His perfect timing, the Lord fulfilled my annual promise to Him to publish my writing, even as I had laid down my own plans and expectations.

• • •

What I could not see at the time was how lovingly God was confirming the lesson He had already taught me: that multiplication always comes through obedience, humility, and shared voice. Before *Voices of ALOHA* would be released to the world, He allowed me to experience what it meant to contribute to something greater than myself—where the message mattered more than the messenger.

That experience sealed the truth in my heart. This movement was never meant to elevate one name. It was always meant to amplify many voices for the glory of God.

The Harmony Beneath the Stories

As these women share their journeys, you may notice a rhythm beneath the words—a pattern that repeats itself in different ways, through different lives. That rhythm is not accidental. It is what we call ALOHA.

ALOHA is more than a word. It is a way of living, healing, and becoming. It is the harmony that allows each voice in this book to sing freely without being forced into uniformity.

* * *

Here is the truth: no story in this anthology belongs to only one part of ALOHA. Healing is never linear. Growth does not happen in neat categories. And testimony is rarely tidy.

Instead, ALOHA moves like music; layered, fluid, and alive.

A — Affirmations & Actions: the quiet moments when a woman chooses to live, to speak truth over herself, or to take one brave step forward even while afraid.

L — Leadership & Love: the realization that leadership often begins in survival, and love; especially God's love—teaches us how to lead ourselves before we lead anyone else.

O — Overcoming Obstacles: the storms that should have silenced these voices but didn't. Abuse, addiction, betrayal, grief, fear, and loss that were confronted rather than denied.

H — Health & Healing: the long, sacred work of restoration: mental, emotional, physical, and spiritual, where scars become signposts instead of shame.

A — Acute Awareness: the awakening. The moment when a woman sees clearly, who she is, whose she is, and why her story matters.

You will hear all of these notes throughout this book. Sometimes they are loud. Sometimes they are barely audible. But together, they create a harmony that points back to the same truth:

God was present in every story—even when it didn't feel like it.

For the Woman Reading This

You may recognize yourself in one voice.

Or in many.

You may see your past reflected in pages you weren't ready to read—or your future hinted at in words that feel like a lifeline. You may find comfort, conviction, courage, or tears you didn't expect.

Whatever rises in you as you read—let it rise.

This is not a book meant to fix you. It is a book meant to remind you.

You are not alone. You are not forgotten. You are not disqualified by what you've survived.

• • •

If these women could sing again after what they've walked through, so can you.

How to Read This Book

Think of each chapter as a solo within a greater song.

Listen for the note that resonates with your heart. Pay attention to where hope flickers. Notice how God weaves redemption differently in every life.

And when you finish a story, pause.

Breathe. Reflect.

Ask yourself:

- Where do I hear my own voice in this?
- Which part of ALOHA is stirring in me right now?
- What might God be inviting me to heal, release, or reclaim?

There is no right order to transformation. There is only willingness.

• • •

A Sacred Beginning

This choir did not gather to perform. It gathered to testify.

Each woman in these pages is a Daughter of the King; not because her life was easy, but because she endured. Because she chose truth over silence. Because she allowed God to meet her in the middle of her story, not just at the end.

May these voices hold you when you feel weary. May they strengthen you when your own voice feels faint. And may you discover, somewhere between their words, the courage to sing again.

Welcome to *Voices of ALOHA: Daughters of the King.*

The song has already begun.

ALOHA INTEGRATION ~

When the Shepherd Goes First

If you felt seen in this story, pause here.

Not because the journey is over, but because something sacred has just begun.

This testimony was not shared to impress you or persuade you. It was offered as an invitation. An open hand saying, *"You are not alone, and you do not have to walk this path unseen."* When a shepherd goes first, it is not to lead with perfection, but with presence.

You may have recognized familiar questions rising in your heart:

- *Am I really hearing God?*
- *Why does obedience sometimes feel harder than resistance?*
- *What if my struggle is actually an invitation to something greater?*

If those questions surface, let them rest gently. God is not threatened by them. In fact, He often uses them as doorways.

As you reflect, notice where ALOHA quietly revealed itself:

• • •

Acute Awareness

There are moments when God interrupts our plans—not to delay us, but to deepen us. Where might He be inviting you to listen more closely rather than push harder?

Leadership & Love

True leadership often begins with surrender. Before platforms, before titles, before clarity, there is obedience. Where might God be asking you to lead yourself with more grace?

Affirmations & Actions

Sometimes faith looks like taking the next small step without knowing the full map. What gentle action feels aligned for you right now; not forced, but faithful?

You are not behind.

You are not late.

You are not failing because the path looks different than you expected.

God is faithful to complete what He begins—even when the assignment changes shape.

Before continuing, offer this simple prayer:

Lord, steady my heart as I listen.
Help me trust You when the way feels unfamiliar.
Give me courage to follow where You lead—one step at a time.
Amen.

When you are ready, turn the page.

Another voice is waiting.
And you are now listening as part of the choir.

E Komo Mai

About the Author: Michelle A. G. Ebalaroza Kawano is a Christian Speaker, Author, and Creative Coach dedicated to helping individuals rediscover their God-given potential and purpose. Born and raised in Hawai'i, Michelle's life and work are deeply influenced by the spirit of ALOHA—living with love, humility, resilience, and awareness.

She is a wife, a mom of four, a proud grandma of eight, and above all, a Daughter of the King. Michelle travels the world with her husband, Bruce, sharing faith, creativity, and testimony while stewarding spaces for connection and transformation.

• • •

Michelle is the award-winning author of *Walking in ALOHA: 5 Steps to Living Your God Potential Life* (2023) and *31 Steps to Mastery: Essential Toolkits for Personal and Professional Success* (2024). Her writing blends Christian faith, lived experience, and practical wisdom to guide readers toward clarity, healing, and purposeful action.

A survivor of domestic violence and a passionate advocate for restoration, Michelle brings a trauma-informed, Christ-centered approach to storytelling and leadership. She believes testimony is not only a pathway to personal healing, but a catalyst for collective transformation and Kingdom impact.

She is the founder of Blessed To Be A Blessing Worldwide Publishing and the visionary behind the Voices of ALOHA movement. Committed to publishing annually as an act of obedience and worship, Michelle continues to honor God as the ultimate Author; restoring voices, honoring stories, and transforming lives one testimony at a time.

Michelle is also the host of the Walking in ALOHA; Let's Talk Story Podcast, where she facilitates real *talk story* conversations that encourage reflection, change, courage, and alignment with purpose and the ALOHA Always framework—connecting guests from all over the world through shared stories and lived

● ● ●

experience. She is the creator and host of ALOHA & Aligned: Women Answer the Call ~ 2026 Virtual International Women's Summit and the ALOHA Always Creative Compendium, bringing together women globally to rise in alignment, leadership, creativity, and calling.

Chapter Two

ALL WAYS

by Amy Colter

I am a very fortunate woman. My mother asked Jesus to care for me when I was born. I truly believe her simple prayer and surrender of her only child to Christ shaped the way I experience life. I have been blessed in so many astounding ways. Every life comes with its trials. It is how we react to them that defines who we are and what will follow. Sometimes. We need to stay aware. But if there's anything I've learned, God is in control. Always.

I was born in Colorado Springs, Colorado. My mother had gone there on vacation and decided to stay. She met my biological father, and I was born. My first memory is actually quite a disturbing one. I will forever despise Tag because when I got caught by my father, he molested me.

We left Colorado to move back east by the time I was three and a half. In that short time, I had almost died of meningitis; our attic had caught fire because of faulty wiring, and the mafia had targeted us because our neighbor was one of their own and had gotten busted. Apparently, they thought my father was an informant. My mom told me we were sent to a hotel for a few days until it was straightened out. We moved soon after to be closer to my maternal grandmother. I've lived in upstate New York ever since.

Once, when I was seven or eight, my biological father took me on a trip. When we got there, I found out his uncle was a pedophile, too. My cousin and I were both victimized. Looking back, it was a form of familial trafficking. That uncle later moved north and became my caregiver while my parents worked.

Things plagued my childhood; no child should have to experience or do. Days of wishing I didn't have to go home, dreading turning the corner to see his truck. He was waiting for me. Then he'd go back to work. I prayed to my real father.

My biological father was building a room in the basement. He had bought a video camera. Afraid, I kicked him one night, telling him to leave me alone, that I was trying to sleep. Then one day I told him "No" when he tried to touch me. He hit me on the arm. He had never hit me before. I told my mother.

At age eleven, the molestation ended. My mother and I left. Its effects, however, are still very present in my psyche. Always will be. The results of trauma. Details of which no one needs to know. I wish I didn't. I am aware others who have been through anything similar will have their own memories to fight now, reading this.

That same winter, my grandmother died. Her home had been my refuge. My father wasn't allowed there. The weekends my mother and I went to visit were the greatest blessings of my childhood. My uncle, who was mentally slow, lived there. He had a dandy train set on an old pool table. My grandmother was a great cook, and I remember listening to polka, dancing cheek-to-cheek, the smell of percolated coffee and Holupke (stuffed cabbage simmering in tomato sauce), with pre-cooked breaded pork chops nestled on top, filling the house. Golly, those were the days. She loved me so, and I her. Watching the color of her skin change as she took her last breath, I "saw" her soul leaving. The death rattle was her body succumbing to its loss of…her. My heart tore in two that day.

School was an awkward endeavor, to say the least. I was bullied and spat on. Made fun of and whispered about. Some kids were nice. Many were not. It was hard to see anyone when my mind had been so disrupted by my home life and circumstances. Even the few I called friends.

Feeling alienated was part of my social experience. Now that I see things differently, I realize part of that was me. I differed from most kids, thankfully so. I didn't talk much. I had gotten used to being quiet and keeping secrets. And I have the knack of saying inappropriate things without meaning to. So I spend a lot of my time doing anything that doesn't have anything to do with people outside family- not that it helps. I simply cling to the flight and save the fight for when I need it.

Growing up, we went to church on Sundays. I heard all the usual stories about Noah and Jonah and Adam and Eve and Cain and Abel. I did my Sunday school lessons and went to service. I was baptized at eight years old. Some lessons made their way into my habits. I tried to be nice to people because I wanted people to be nice to me. I didn't steal, not just because I knew it was wrong, but because I didn't like things being stolen from me. But many of the lessons took a lot longer for me to absorb. Like keeping the Sabbath, which is from sunset Friday to sunset Saturday. Sunday church doesn't click with me anymore. Keeping The Commandments does.

I also had a recurring dream as a child. From when I was very young until the age of fourteen, when I painted a rendition of it. The dream was me, on a white sand desert that was reflecting the lilac color of the sky. I jump into a man-made pool, indicative of life's journey. Lightning illuminates the sky, and I get out of the water as an earthquake shakes mountains into existence in the distance. The storms forming over the mountains strike them with massive bolts of lightning, one of which opens a volcano. A white-blue, brightly glowing cross emerges from the lava spew. Then a dagger, which attaches to the bottom of the cross. Then a white light that reveals a green, perfect earth through a porthole. The white light overtakes me, and I wake.

It would be easy to think I was affected by my years of attending church, but I was too young to have heard all of that. The dream started soon after my first memory- the horrible one with my father- at the age of three. And somehow, I have always known it was God's way of telling me that I would witness the revolution of Jesus in this lifetime. Something opened my eyes very early.

Life happened in the usual way. Time passes, and we have experiences and make choices. I tried college, flunked myself out. Fell in love, fell out of love. Made friends I regrettably lost. Throughout that time, I had found a fascination in theology. I had started praying to God when I was little, mostly to end the abuse. Sometimes The Lord's Prayer. But that was where the questions started. Was my belief in Jesus only a result of being taught it? Was I deluding myself when I thought maybe the Holy Spirit was guiding me? Was I saying "Thank You" to no one? Why were there so many religions, many with similarities that spanned thousands of years? Is one right? Is there really a God?

The first of very clear answers was presented when I came upon a Ouija board. I was twenty. It was in a closet at my friend's house. I put the box on the floor and sat, reaching for the box. It suddenly felt as if a tornado had formed around me. The room didn't exist anymore. A booming voice said, "That is not meant for you."

Needless to say, I didn't open the box. I shoved it back into the closet and promptly exited. In an odd coincidence, we didn't remain friends. I didn't tell anyone for fear they would think I was crazy. Sad that when the Lord speaks, we can be afraid to proclaim it. In the years that followed, I had become curious about learning Wicca versus witchcraft, ghosts, astrology, and tarot. I see these things as being manipulated by nefarious forces. I thought I should know my enemies.

There was a cafe with great coffee that had regular tarot readings. The person doing my reading said something about my

● ● ●

grandmother, how she was there with me, that she said something about spaghetti and laughed. I felt a cold pressure on my right shoulder. But I could sense it wasn't my grandmother. And there would have been no reason for her to laugh. We had comforting dinners every Sunday, usually pasta of some sort, yes. But the laughing didn't make sense. That confirmed to me that there was something off. Nausea had formed a knot in my stomach when whatever it was touched me. I left and had a better understanding of such things. And that "They are not meant for" me.

Everything is connected, if only by the simple fact that it exists. Everything has energy, which cannot be destroyed, only transferred or transformed. Acknowledging that demons and devils exist comes with acknowledging that angels and Christ exist. All of which, whether we can see them or not, are composed by The Creator, who rearranges the puzzle pieces of existence every time every person uses free will or utilizes prayer.

Learning comes from everywhere. I learned to be extremely aware of cross-contamination by being a dental assistant. I learned how to speak in a kind manner because I hurt my mother with my attitude. I learned to watch what I was doing and how it would affect others when I hurt my friends without thinking.

• • •

Being an introvert means doing a lot of observing and not a lot of talking. I have prayed so much that I find myself venting and praying and spinning off all at once in quiet chaos. Having the tendency to put my foot in my mouth has also prompted me to attempt to speak only with positive purpose. We're all human, and I still blurt. But on the plus side, I have taken these opportunities to embrace things like compassion, empathy, and mindfulness. Listening: combining it with hearing. And patience. I am still learning patience.

I also learned that when Mary said her son's name, it would not be said "Jesus". So, I try to say His name as His mother would have- Yeshua. When I remember to. I've been calling Him Jesus for a very long time.

As I said, I have been blessed. I have good memories to keep in my pocket. My mother raised me with manners and morals. Ethics and ethos. I have made mistakes and still feel bad for things I have done or wish I had not. But guilt wastes time. It can even prevent us from learning whatever lesson we were meant to learn. From seeing and taking responsibility for our actions to forgiving ourselves and correcting our behaviors. Apathy proves as useless as anger. Fighting the love that we were created with is self-sabotage.

● ● ●

Ripples are made from both kindness and cruelty. Depression is a battle within that can affect our without. Like a river of feelings and thoughts, let them come, let them pass. Make them pass. Choose to be present. Dwelling in sorrow only keeps time from dulling the pain that comes with it. I remind myself to be a duck- let the rain roll off my back. Let it go. Easier said than done.

It's not easy to be consistently and constantly aware. When I step out into the world, I am watching other people and myself, minding body language and mannerisms, understanding vocal tones and facial expressions define what is being said, knowing they can be deceiving. We never really know anyone, even ourselves, until presented with choices and circumstances. Like a person who is a friend to some, but a terrorist to others. Or someone who has been through more than would be imagined. Or the pedophiles who can't hide their eyes from me but seem to from everyone else.

Then there's driving. Road safety is a whole other endeavor where being aware and active prayer are paramount. Yeshua once kept a car working until I could get my sick son to the hospital. It died as soon as we parked in the driveway. Prayer works! Praise Yeshua!

Keeping our eyes open, figuratively, is one of the most important steps we can take toward mindfulness. Mindfulness can take life in

• • •

directions we may not have otherwise seen. Or save us from certain demise. It kept me from being kidnapped. Casual observation can facilitate understanding. It's when we don't look that we don't see.

Like getting frustrated when we haven't asked for help. There is no martyrdom in silent suffering. Just loneliness and pain, building upon themselves in our hearts. Darkening our sight and taking our grip on the truth- that we exist for a reason. We are important. Created to be divinely loved.

A few years ago, I started having cravings. I'm not physically in a position to have another child. I knew I was pregnant, even though I never took a test. I knew it was not Yeshua's will for me to have an abortion. I was scared. I prayed that if either of us were going to die as a result of pregnancy or childbirth, please not let it be.

A peace came over me. Yeshua took the fear. A few days later, I was in bed with abdominal pain. By the end of the day, I had miscarried. I realize Yeshua had probably saved my life, but I still mourn. Every time I see what I craved in the grocery store or a newborn. The child might not have made it either. My pain is nothing compared to the sorrows I may not have been able to psychologically survive. I am ever so thankful for the boldness of The Saviour.

• • •

The only things that matter are those we take with us when we die. Our memories, our character, and our choices. Karmic retribution from our life on earth will roll over at the time of judgement. The Consciousness of Existence always has been and always will be. Without motion in some direction, there would be nothing. Molecules of a rock still move.

Though there are some days depression descends, pulling the dark wool over my soul, where I wish I didn't exist, I can always come back with the fact that I refuse to commit suicide, though it took me years to fully reject the notion, and may take hours to think to.

Faith helps. Yeshua helps. To fight, or to succumb. We will exist after this life. Who we have been in this one matters. How we are to others matters. Our countenance matters. Whether we acknowledge The Creator through The Christ matters. There is nothing that doesn't matter. There are some things we should take heed to keep of most import, if not for ourselves, for the sake of all that is, and all that will be. We have an effect. Whether we like it or know it or not. To be present and mindful. To always thank Yeshua for that loaf of bread He left in the back of the shelf for you, and for the bad day you've had. Remind yourself: He's got you. One way or another. All ways, always.

"Thou shalt love the Lord thy God with all thy heart, and with all thy soul, and with all thy mind." ~Matthew 22:37

• • •

28

ALOHA INTEGRATION ~

When Awareness Became Protection

If this story stirred something old or tender in you, pause here.

Some wounds form before we have words.
Some fears take root before we understand what safety feels like.
And some awareness; the kind that keeps us alert, observant, watchful;
is not weakness at all. It is wisdom born of survival.

If you recognized yourself in this story, know this first and clearly:

You are not "too sensitive."
You are not imagining what your spirit has learned to discern.
God has been near you longer than you have had language to name
Him.

As you reflect, notice how ALOHA moved quietly through this
testimony:

Acute Awareness
God sometimes sharpens our awareness not to burden us, but to protect
us. Where have you learned to notice what others overlook and how
might God be inviting you to trust that discernment without living in
fear?

• • •

Health & Healing

Healing does not erase memory. It redeems it. Where might God be teaching you to tend your inner world with compassion rather than judgment?

Leadership & Love

Leading does not always look like speaking loudly. Sometimes it looks like choosing gentleness, boundaries, and truth; again and again. How might love be guiding you to care for yourself more faithfully? If emotions surfaced as you read; grief, anger, confusion, relief, let them be what they are. God does not rush healing, and He does not demand explanations before offering comfort.

Before you turn the page, rest in this prayer:

God of refuge,
You saw me when I learned to be alert.
You guarded me when I could not guard myself.
Teach me now how to live aware, but not afraid,
present, but not burdened.
I place what I cannot carry into Your hands.
Amen.

About the Author: Amy Colter is a woman of faith whose life reflects resilience, discernment, and a deep love for God. Guided by the words of Matthew 22:37—*"Thou shalt love the Lord thy God with all thy heart, and with all thy soul and with all thy mind"*—Amy's journey has been shaped by learning to listen closely to God's presence, even in seasons that required great awareness and quiet strength.

Through her testimony, Amy shares how God met her in formative experiences, gently leading her toward healing, self-compassion, and trust. Her story honors the truth that sensitivity can become

• • •

wisdom, awareness can become protection, and faith can grow steadily, even when it develops in silence.

Amy lives in upstate New York with her loving and supportive family. She is married to Peter Colter, who is also a contributing author in *Voices of ALOHA: Mighty Men of God*. Together, they value faith, family, and the power of testimony.

Amy is currently working toward the release of her first and only novel, which she hopes to publish by the end of next year. By sharing her story in *Voices of ALOHA: Daughters of the King*, Amy's prayer is that readers will feel seen, encouraged, and reminded that God has been near them all along.

Chapter 3

NOT BROKEN...YOU JUST HAVEN'T FOUND IT YET

By: Jennifer Kotel

The Missing Piece

For years I checked every box that was supposed to add up to a good life.

I built businesses. I earned a steady paycheck. I got married. I raised a family.

On the outside, it looked like I had everything anyone could want.

On the inside, there was a quiet whisper in the back of my mind: Is this all there is?

I couldn't explain it. I only knew something was missing — not from my circumstances, but from me.

• • •

That ache shaped far more of my choices than I realized and almost convinced me to stay small, quiet, unseen.

The Weight of Loss

I know what it feels like to watch something you've built wash away.

I learned that in 2004, when the tsunami hit Southeast Asia.

At the time, my parents had a nutritional-supplement company that my mom helped bring to the Philippines. My dad, I, and a small team were expanding it into Malaysia.

I had begged my mom and dad to let me stay in Malaysia for the holidays and move back after. A group of friends was planning a trip to Phuket for Christmas and New Years. They insisted on me coming home. That morning, I remember the phone call from my dad telling me to turn on the news. I remember sitting in front of the TV, the blue glow lighting the room as the news continued to show footage of the waves rolling in. I watched in disbelief, realizing the magnitude of what had happened. Not only did I lose some great friends, but I realized that my business was going to suffer. It's hard to believe what my fate would have been if I had stayed.

Years later, another wave hit — this time, it was COVID-19.

By then I'd built an online-marketing company serving small businesses that relied heavily on walk-in customers. When the world shut down, so did their revenue streams, and in a matter of months my business collapsed too.

I told myself I was strong enough to rebuild again, but in the quiet moments I wondered: How many more times can I start over?

After that second loss, I chose safety: a corporate job with a steady paycheck and benefits.

On paper, it made perfect sense; in my heart, it cost more than I expected: missed dinners, missed school moments, missed the kind of presence I'd always promised my family I'd give them.

Even marriage and motherhood, as beautiful as they were, couldn't silence that lingering question: Is this it?

● ● ●

Early Sparks of a Dream

Long before those losses, I'd had glimpses of a different path.

Years earlier, I'd attended a weekend self-development course.

I walked in curious and left changed; lighter, clearer, hopeful in a way I hadn't felt for years.

On the last afternoon, I sat in the back row, notebook on my lap, watching the facilitator on stage. Something in me stirred:

I want to do what they're doing. I want to help people feel this shift too.

That was the first time the dream of speaking lit up inside me.

I even signed up for the leadership track, convinced I'd found my purpose.

But part of the training required recruiting new participants. Cold-calling strangers terrified me; every "no" felt personal. Eventually fear won, and I backed away.

Later I tried another avenue: I entered Miss Illinois USA and Ms. Petit International Pageants.

From the outside, it may have looked like I was chasing crowns, but it was never about a sash. I wanted a platform to speak for women who'd survived abuse; women I longed to tell, You are worth more than what happened to you.

I prepared and showed up, but comparison crept in. Surrounded by polished, confident contestants, I thought, Who am I to belong here?

When I didn't win, I tucked the dream away again.

Looking back, I see those weren't failures; they were seeds of the same desire: to stand on a stage, use my voice, and help others believe in their worth.

Meeting the Mentors → Spark

What finally reignited that dream were the people whose lives embodied courage in different forms.

My mom was my first example of quiet strength.

She came to the United States from the Philippines before she was eighteen, leaving behind everything familiar to start over in a country where she didn't know a soul.

For years she taught piano lessons out of our living room to help support the family.

But she never stopped learning or reaching higher; she eventually earned her Master's degree at Northwestern and later a PhD at Mundelein.

I watched her go from a teenage immigrant piano teacher to the owner of her own international business.

Growing up with that example taught me that resilience doesn't always roar; sometimes it simply keeps showing up and finding a way forward.

Then there was Tony Robbins.

For more than twenty years, I attended his seminars, filling notebooks until my hand cramped.

Watching him command a room didn't just motivate me; it reminded me of the part of myself I'd kept hiding, the part that wanted to inspire others too.

● ● ●

And yes… Taylor Swift.

You may love her or be tired of hearing her name, but what struck me wasn't the fame; it was the courage.

She faces critics daily and still shows up to sing her truth.

That taught me that critics don't get the final word.

I didn't want to be them.

I wanted to be my own version of them.

For the first time in a long time, I believed I could.

That was the Spark.

Crossing the Threshold → Stoke the Flame

A spark fades unless you feed it.

I started quietly; journaling when my words felt clumsy, gratitude lists when I wanted to dwell on loss, whispered prayers asking God for courage.

Little by little, I began saying it out loud: "I want to be a speaker."

• • •

At first, it sounded foreign coming from my own mouth, but the more I said it, the more real it became.

Finally, I took the step that terrified me most: I entered the Next Top Speaker competition.

I remember hovering over the Submit button with my mouse, my hand trembling.

My inner critic screamed, "You're not ready. You'll embarrass yourself."

But another voice whispered back: "You've been stuck long enough. It's time to try."

That whisper — not the fear — was the one I chose to follow.

That was me learning to Stoke the Flame.

The Ordeal → Set on Fire

I pictured my audition video being confident and polished.

Instead… I ugly-cried.

Not a soft, movie-scene tear; a full, unplanned, blotchy-faced cry.

For a moment, I thought I'd ruined everything.

But in that raw, unguarded moment, I discovered something I'd missed all along: people don't connect with perfect; they connect with real.

That video, the one I almost deleted; earned me a place in the Top 100 out of 3,000 speakers… then the Top 50.

I didn't win the trophy, but I found something better: I found my voice.

That was the moment I truly set all my fears and negative thoughts about failure on fire.

Reward and the Road Back

Not winning the trophy could have felt like defeat — and not too long ago, it probably would have.

Instead, I saw it as proof that showing up as my authentic self mattered more than any award.

Share the Gift → Return with the Elixir

Here's what I learned:

Courage doesn't arrive after you succeed; it grows the moment you say yes to yourself, even while you're still scared.

Sometimes the missing piece isn't out in the world at all.

Sometimes it's already inside you, waiting for you to stop hiding and take the first brave, imperfect step.

If you are struggling to come up with something,

You're not broken…

You Just Haven't Found It Yet

Your Next Step

Before you move on to the next story, pause for one minute.

Grab a scrap of paper or open the Notes app on your phone.

Write down the one "whisper" you've been ignoring; that quiet thought that says, There's more for me than this.

● ● ●

You don't have to solve it yet. Just name it.

Change often begins the moment we give that whisper a voice.

Then, before the next 24 hours pass, take one small, brave step toward it. Send an email, make a call, or simply tell someone you trust.

Tiny sparks become flames when we act on them.

A Final Word

If this story stirred something in you — that quiet whisper that says there's more for you — I'd love to hear about it.

You can find me at www.mental-ninjas.com or on Instagram @EmpowHER_Ninja.

Sometimes sharing the whisper is the very first spark.

Scripture Reflection

Joshua 1:9– "Have I not commanded you? Be strong and courageous. Do not be afraid; do not be discouraged, for the Lord your God will be with you wherever you go."

• • •

ALOHA INTEGRATION ~

When the Quiet Whisper Refused to Leave

If this story felt familiar, pause here.

Some callings don't arrive with thunder.
They come as a whisper you try to ignore.
A nudge you explain away.
A longing that won't quiet, no matter how full your life appears on the outside.

If you have ever thought, *"I should be grateful—so why do I still feel like there's more?"*
You are not unfaithful.
You are not ungrounded.
You may simply be listening.

As you reflect, notice how ALOHA unfolded gently through this story:

Affirmations & Actions

Sometimes courage looks like naming what you want—first to yourself, then to God. Where might He be inviting you to take one honest step, even if it feels imperfect or unfinished?

• • •

Leadership & Love

Leadership does not always begin on a stage. Often it starts with the willingness to stop shrinking your voice. Where might love be asking you to lead by showing up as your true self?

Acute Awareness

There are moments when clarity doesn't shout—it settles. What truth about who you are felt unmistakable as you read?

Loss, disappointment, and fear have a way of convincing us that dreams were meant for someone else. But God does not place desires in our hearts to tease us. He places them there to draw us forward.

You are not behind because you took the long way.
You are not disqualified because you paused.
And you are not foolish for wanting a life that feels aligned.

Before turning the page, offer this prayer:

God who sees the unseen,
Help me trust the whisper You placed in me.
Give me courage to stop dismissing what You keep repeating.
Teach me to move forward without needing every answer.
Amen.

● ● ●

About the Author: Jennifer "Jen" Kotel lives with her husband, Jim, their son, Max, and their Boston Terrier, Leo. Based in Chicago, Illinois, she is a motivational speaker, mental health and confidence coach, and the founder of EmpowHER Effect Co., as well as co-founder of Mental Ninjas. Through her work, Jen equips women with practical tools and mindset strategies to rebuild confidence, strengthen emotional resilience, and rediscover their worth.

Her journey reflects resilience, courage, and attentiveness to the quiet whisper of God's calling. Having navigated seasons of loss and rebuilding, Jen shares how moments of collapse became invitations to rediscover purpose, reclaim her voice, and move forward one faithful step at a time.

Rooted in authenticity and empowerment, she is passionate about helping women trust the whispers placed in their hearts and step boldly into the life they were created for. By contributing her story to *Voices of ALOHA: Daughters of the King*, she hopes readers will be reminded that longing for more may simply mean God is calling them forward.

Chapter 4

DEAR YOUNGER ME: FROM CHAOS TO CLARITY

By: Felicia S. Collins

The Breaking Point

There was a season when I woke up every morning wondering how much more I could take. Divorce papers sat on the counter, bills formed a choir of reminders, and three pairs of eyes looked up at me for answers I didn't have. One of my daughters needed constant medical attention, and I carried my own invisible wounds—PTSD and MST that haunted my sleep.

People whispered their opinions as if they were facts: "She can't handle all that." "Single moms never get far." I tried to prove them wrong, but my body and spirit were running on fumes.

When everything collapsed, it wasn't quiet. It was a full-blown, ugly cry—knees on the floor, heart in pieces, whispering, "God, help me."

● ● ●

And He did. Just not all at once.

The Turning Point

Six months of homelessness felt like living in a holding pattern between despair and determination. I learned to make "temporary" feel like "home," and I learned how heavy hope can feel when it's all you have left.

Then one night, I broke—loudly. I screamed and sobbed until the surrounding air stilled. That was the first time I truly surrendered.

Soon after, I joined an online women's group. I barely typed a sentence at first—just little crumbs of truth—but those crumbs became a feast of healing. These women didn't judge my cracks; they showed me where light could enter.

Healing started there, quietly, through connection, prayer, and the realization that even in brokenness, God still had a plan.

• • •

The Climb

Once stability returned—a set of house keys that jingled like freedom—I began climbing. I enrolled in courses, started writing again, and prepared to resign from a job that no longer matched the woman I was becoming.

Right before turning in my notice, a stranger stopped me in the parking lot. "You have such a beautiful light," she said. "You were made to help others. You have a purpose."

I smiled politely, but inside I froze. That woman had just spoken the words my soul needed most. Confirmation delivered by an angel in sneakers.

Not long after, a friend invited me to Dubai for her 45th birthday. I almost said no—because moms don't "just fly to Dubai," right? But something in me whispered, Go.

And oh, I went. I laughed until my cheeks hurt, cried in awe at sunsets over the desert, and realized how small my fears had become next to God's horizon. Somewhere between camel rides and rooftop dinners, clarity bloomed.

When I came back home, I wasn't the same. I was ready to act, to build, to bloom.

• • •

And yes—somewhere between that revelation and homeschooling Makaio (who was definitely supposed to be working on his laptop but was secretly playing games on his tablet while Lego bricks staged a battlefield across the floor)—I realized I didn't need perfection to walk in purpose. I just needed obedience and a sense of humor.

The Blooming

Faith doesn't erase the hard things; it gives them meaning.

I founded Bailey Global: Women of Worth (WOW) to help other women find what I almost lost—their worth. My goal wasn't to impress; it was to impact. To show women that clarity isn't the absence of chaos—it's peace within it.

Through coaching, writing, and speaking, I watched broken women remember who they were. I've seen tears turn into testimonies and fear morph into leadership.

Leadership, I've learned, is an act of love—first for yourself, then for others.

● ● ●

The Lessons

Looking back, I see God's fingerprints everywhere.

He brought me through trauma so I could guide others out of theirs.

He taught me to let go of control, shame, and the need to prove my worth.

He reminded me that my story is meant to reach the woman who thinks she's disqualified from destiny.

To that woman I would say: Don't believe the lies. You are still chosen. The storm was never meant to drown you—it was meant to teach you to walk on water.

Everything I lost became the soil where my purpose grew.

The Message

Dear woman reading this, I know life can feel like chaos wearing a name tag that says "responsibility." I know what it's like to pray for miracles while reheating coffee three times because motherhood doesn't wait.

But hear me—your story isn't over. The same God who met me in shelters, classrooms, therapy sessions, and airports is waiting to meet you too.

Healing doesn't mean forgetting. It means you no longer bleed from the wound. It means you use your scars as signposts for someone else's way home.

Faith Reflection

Habakkuk 2:3 (AMP)

"For the vision is yet for the appointed time;

it hurries toward the goal [of fulfillment]; it will not fail.

Even though it delays, wait [patiently] for it,

Because it will certainly come; it will not delay."

For years, I thought my vision was buried under bills, broken trust, and burnout. But God reminded me—it was just waiting for its appointed time.

The Call to Action – Flourish with Grace

If my story stirs something in you, don't ignore it. That's the sound of purpose knocking.

Bailey Global: Women of Worth was born from that same knock. It's a safe space where women heal, grow, and rediscover their worth through faith and sisterhood. Join us. Let's rebuild your confidence, reawaken your vision, and activate your worth— together.

Because the world needs your light, and somebody's healing depends on your "yes."

Closing Encouragement / Prayer

Father, thank You for every woman reading this. For the one barely hanging on, remind her she's seen. For the one ready to rise, give her courage to move. And for the one walking in purpose, teach her to reach back and lift another. Turn our chaos into clarity, our pain into power, and help us flourish—with grace.

Amen.

ALOHA INTEGRATION ~

When God Meets You in the Middle of Survival

If this story left you feeling tired in your bones, pause here.

Some seasons don't allow space for reflection while you're living them. You are too busy surviving. Too responsible to fall apart. Too needed to rest. And yet, God does not wait for the chaos to settle before He draws near.

If you saw yourself in this story juggling responsibility, carrying invisible wounds, showing up even when you felt empty; hear this gently:

God has never overlooked your endurance.

You may not have had the luxury of stopping. You may not have had time to heal neatly or process fully. But faith lived under pressure is still faith and God honors it.

As you reflect, notice how ALOHA carried you through this story:

Overcoming Obstacles
Survival required strength you didn't ask for. What once felt like evidence of brokenness may now reveal resilience God was building all along.

• • •

Health & Healing

Healing does not always begin when life becomes calm. Often, it begins when someone finally sees you and says, *"You don't have to do this alone anymore."* Where might God be inviting you to receive support instead of pushing through?

Leadership & Love

Leadership sometimes looks like showing up tired and choosing love anyway. How might God be asking you to lead yourself with the same compassion you give everyone else?

If guilt surfaced as you read about rest you didn't take, choices made in exhaustion, or moments you wish you could redo; release it. God does not shame women who carried families, homes, and futures while bleeding quietly.

Before continuing, sit with this prayer:

God who sees the unseen labor,
Thank You for meeting me where I was; not where I wished I could be.
Restore what survival required me to set aside.
Teach me how to rest without fear and trust without striving.
Amen.

About the Author: Felicia S. Collins is a Christ-follower, speaker, coach, and purpose-driven entrepreneur based in Jennings, Florida. A medically retired U.S. Army veteran, Felicia's life has been shaped by perseverance through trauma, homelessness, single motherhood, and healing—experiences that now anchor her calling to help other women rise with faith and clarity.

She is the Founder and Coach of Bailey Global: Women of Worth (WOW) LLC, a faith-centered community created to help women heal, grow, and rediscover their worth. Felicia is also the owner of Flourishing with Grace, a permanent and customized jewelry brand through JBloom. As a speaker, she has been featured with

• • •

100 Speakers alongside Kaley Chu, sharing messages of leadership, restoration, and purpose.

Felicia is a proud mother of three—Leanna (19), Aiyanna (15), and Makaio (8)—and finds joy in time spent with her children and close relatives, traveling, speaking, volunteering, and building community among women worldwide.

Rooted deeply in her faith, Felicia believes that clarity is not the absence of chaos, but peace within it. Through coaching, storytelling, and service, she empowers women to transform pain into purpose, embrace leadership with love, and activate their God-given worth. By contributing her story to *Voices of ALOHA: Daughters of the King*, Felicia hopes readers are reminded that they are still chosen—and that healing, leadership, and grace can flourish even after the hardest seasons.

Chapter 5

TO HIM, THROUGH HIM

A Testimony of Redemption, Healing, and Purpose

By: Bri-Anne Banglos

My husband and I both come from divorced families. Because of that, neither of us knew what a healthy marriage relationship looked like.

When I was seven, I watched my mother's heart shatter when my father—her high school sweetheart and the love of her life—left her for another woman. I made a vow to myself that I would never end up like her: heartbroken, abandoned, and vulnerable.

My husband, Phil, never really knew his father. His dad left when he was two, and he was raised mostly by women. He had an older brother, but he was often gone, so Phil grew up without a strong

● ● ●

male role model. Neither of us grew up in homes centered on Christ. I attended Catholic school until sixth grade, and Phil occasionally went to church with his aunt, but faith wasn't a consistent part of our lives.

When we met on September 20, 2006, we were both in our early twenties and already parents. I had two children, ages five and six, from a volatile, addiction-fueled relationship with my high school sweetheart. Phil had two young boys, ages one and two, from an on-again, off-again relationship.

We met at a bar in Kapolei. I was out with my best friend, who was going through a divorce at the time—both of us just out to "have a good time," trying to fill our emptiness with distraction. Phil was supposed to be just a one-night stand, but we kept in touch and started seeing each other more often—countless nights of partying and sharing drunken conversations about the future. I never took those plans seriously because this wasn't supposed to be anything serious. Yet by January 2007, Phil had moved in with my family and me.

A few months later, in May 2007, I found out I was pregnant. I didn't feel ready. We were still in a season of partying—lost, broken, and far from God. I told Phil I didn't want to bring another child into our chaos, but he begged me to keep the baby, saying he wanted the chance to be a full-time father. So, we decided to try to blend our families and build something new together.

But our foundation was built on lies. Behind my back, Phil resumed a relationship with his ex in early 2007—around the same time I had gotten pregnant. His ex even went out of her way to befriend me, saying she wanted to get to know me since I would be around her children—all while still sleeping with Phil.

Our son, Blaze, was born prematurely on September 23, 2007, weighing only 3 lbs. 12 oz. He was diagnosed with VACTERL syndrome, a rare condition with multiple anomalies. Caring for a child with special needs while raising two kids in elementary school and trying to hold together a broken relationship was overwhelming.

The truth about Phil's affair came out just after Blaze's first birthday. I was crushed. My ex had cheated constantly, and now I found myself reliving that same pain—questioning my worth, blaming myself, and wrestling with wounds that traced all the way back to my father's abandonment.

Still, we tried to fix things. We joined a program called Healthy Marriages through an organization named Keiki o ka ʻĀina, and for a time, it seemed like we were healing. I even reconciled with

Phil's ex so he could see his children again. But in 2010, while I was coping with the decline of my father's health due to a terminal illness, Phil's ex confessed that he had tried to pursue her again. Phil denied it for almost a year until one night he finally admitted the truth. I was exhausted and emotionally done.

I gave Phil an ultimatum: he needed to establish hard boundaries with his ex and children, or he needed to leave. I didn't think it was fair to force my kids to accept his children when I felt used by both Phil and his ex as a dependable babysitter. Phil chose to tell his ex that he never wanted to see her or his kids again.

My father passed away in February 2011, and just a year later, Phil was diagnosed with cancer. Our relationship was hanging by a thread. Phil underwent surgery and started chemotherapy. The kids and I threw ourselves into extracurricular activities: archery, football, baseball, basketball, volleyball, mixed martial arts; anything to cope in a healthier way.

While Phil battled cancer, he developed an addiction to painkillers. I numbed myself with busyness. If I wasn't working or running the kids around, I was drinking and smoking excessively, justifying it because I was "so busy." Our home was filled with tension. Phil and I would often go months without talking, and our children were growing up in dysfunction. My best friend often stepped in to help; running the kids to appointments, practices, and school events, as we tried to hold life together.

By 2016, our older children were in high school, and our youngest was finishing elementary school. My best friend and I found a financial opportunity that focused on personal growth, and through that, God began stirring something in me. I started taking ownership of my part in our declining relationship. I began apologizing to Phil for the toxic, drunken arguments that would often occur when I drank heavily.

By 2018, our two oldest had graduated. The drinking lessened significantly, and Phil began his journey toward sobriety from painkillers. Yet something was still missing, something only the Lord could fill.

In 2019, the Lord opened a door for me to become an eligibility worker in Waianae; a stable state job that allowed me to be present for my youngest child. It also connected me to Joy, a coworker who loves Jesus. She and I remain close to this day. Joy gave me a Bible, prayed with me, encouraged me to go to church, and lovingly corrected my worldly thinking with biblical truth. By this time, I only drank on special occasions, and Phil and I started having honest conversations about our future.

• • •

In September 2020, Phil and I finally moved out of my parents' home into our own place. Then, on October 30, 2020, my oldest son told me he was in love with my best friend. That was my breaking point. I felt completely heartbroken, like everyone I had ever loved had either abandoned or betrayed me. I realized I had become exactly what I swore I wouldn't: heartbroken, abandoned, and vulnerable. I didn't know how to cope anymore as I moved toward total sobriety, but deep down, I knew the only one who could take away that pain was God.

Through that heartbreak, the Lord revealed the truth: every sin, every poor decision, every person I had allowed or removed from my life had brought me to this moment; to the end of myself, where only He could rebuild me, because ultimately, it wasn't about me.

I started attending church again, bringing Blaze with me (he didn't have a choice!). Soon, my daughter and her boyfriend at the time joined us. We all started getting involved at church; first with Alpha Class, then in my first connect group hosted by my Alpha teacher, Cathy. Watching my daughter and her boyfriend find community and grow in faith filled me with gratitude.

During that same time, the Lord helped restore my relationship with my son and his wife. Amazingly, they had also started going to church. Over time, Phil noticed the change in all of us. Without pressure, just consistent love, peace, and joy; he eventually decided to come too. Soon, attending church became part of our routine, and as we got to know people, we began serving in different ministries.

In December 2021, my daughter introduced me to Ju, and by January 2022, Phil and I joined our first couple's connect group. When our leaders, Ju and Mark, learned we had been together for fifteen years but were never married, they lovingly called us out on it. We explained our lack of understanding of marriage's importance, shaped by the pain of divorce in our families.

But through that connection, Phil found a true friend and mentor in Mark, and I found one in Ju; and that changed everything. On February 14, 2022, we got engaged. On March 26, 2022, we were baptized. And on April 1, 2022, we were married by Ju. This time, with a deep yearning to put God at the center; surrounded by all our children, siblings, and parents, we made our covenant before the Lord.

On March 31, 2023, we purchased our first home, a condo in Mililani. In May 2023, we began leading a family group in our home, then Phil finally joined a few men's groups trying to find his fit. In Fall of 2024 we joined our first marriage discipleship group

● ● ●

hosted by Mark and Ju to truly understand God's design for marriage. We made a vow: this marriage will be our only one because what we could not do without God, we can now do through Him.

Since then, we've continued to immerse ourselves in ministry, leadership, and discipleship. Today, we lead a marriage connect group, helping other couples align their relationships with God's purpose. It is an honor to serve and to testify that He restores all things. I also lead a women's Bible study group, and Phil leads a men's 33 Series.

Our oldest children are both married young adults, and we rejoice knowing they understand the sacredness and purpose of the marriage covenant. The Holy Spirit has taught us to see the goodness in every situation—and to trust that God's plan is always better than ours.

What the enemy meant for destruction, God has used for His glory.

Our story is not one of perfection, but of redemption. A living testimony that all things truly work together for good, to Him and through Him.

• • •

The Lord has truly demonstrated Romans 12:1-18 (NLT) in my life; will you allow him to do the same for you?

1 And so, dear brothers and sisters, I plead with you to give your bodies to God because of all he has done for you. Let them be a living and holy sacrifice, the kind he will find acceptable. This is truly the way to worship Him. 2 Don't copy the behavior and customs of this world, but let God transform you into a new person by changing the way you think. Then you will learn to know God's will for you, which is good and pleasing and perfect. 3 Because of the privilege and authority God has given me, I give each of you this warning: Don't think you are better than you really are. Be honest in your evaluation of yourselves, measuring yourselves by the faith God has given us. 4 Just as our bodies have many parts and each part has a special function, 5 so it is with Christ's body. We are many parts of one body, and we all belong to each other.

6 In his grace, God has given us different gifts for doing certain things well. So if God has given you the ability to prophesy, speak out with as much faith as God has given you. 7 If your gist is serving others, serve them well. If you are a teacher, teach well. 8 If your gift is to encourage others, be encouraging. If it is giving, give generously. If God had given you leadership ability, take

• • •

responsibility seriously. And if you have a gift for showing kindness to others, do it gladly.

9 Don't just pretend to love others. Really love them. Hate what is wrong. Hold tightly to what is good. 10 Love each other with genuine affection, and take delight in honoring each other. 11 Never be lazy, but work hard and serve the Lord enthusiastically. 12 Rejoice in our confident hope. Be patient in trouble and keep on praying. 13 When God's people are in need, be ready to help them. Always be eager to practice hospitality. 14 Bless those who persecute you. Don't curse them; pray that God will bless them. 15 Be happy with those who are happy, and weep with those who are happy, and weep with those who weep. 16 Live in harmony with each other. Don't be too proud to enjoy the company of ordinary people. And don't think you know it all!

17 Never pay back evil with more evil. Do things in such a way that everyone can see you are honorable. 18 Do all that you can do to live in; peace with everyone.

The Lord has placed it on my heart to inspire, equip, and empower others to take action that impacts lives. I didn't know at the time how God would bring that mission to fruition, but I chose to follow His lead—and the journey so far has been nothing short of amazing.

* * *

ALOHA INTEGRATION ~

When Love Learned to Stay

If this story stirred something deep in you, pause here.

Some healing does not arrive suddenly.
It comes slowly—through hard conversations, repeated choices, and the quiet decision to stay when leaving would be easier. This story is not about perfection. It is about faithfulness. And faithfulness, when surrendered to God, changes everything.

If you recognized yourself in this journey—loving imperfectly, rebuilding trust, learning what covenant truly means—hear this truth gently:

God is not intimidated by the messiness of restoration.

As you reflect, notice how ALOHA unfolded through this testimony:

Leadership & Love
Love is not proven by intensity, but by consistency. Leadership in relationship often begins when someone chooses humility over pride and truth over comfort. Where might God be inviting you to lead with patience rather than control?

Health & Healing
Healing within relationship takes time. It requires unlearning old

• • •

patterns and allowing God to redefine what safety and partnership look like. Where do you sense God restoring—not just individuals, but connection itself?

Affirmations & Actions

Redemption is built through daily decisions—small, faithful steps taken again and again. What choice might God be asking you to make today that honors the future He is building, even if it feels slow?

If you felt grief for what was lost, or longing for what has yet to be fully restored, let that sit without judgment. God does not rush covenant. He strengthens it.

Before turning the page, rest in this prayer:

God of restoration,
Teach me to trust Your timing.
Heal what was broken, rebuild what was shaken,
and help me choose love the way You do—faithfully, patiently, and with hope.
Amen.

.

About the Author: Bri-Anne Banglos is a woman of faith whose life reflects redemption, perseverance, and a deep commitment to God's design for marriage and family. Her journey has been shaped by early experiences of brokenness, blended-family challenges, and years of relational rebuilding—ultimately leading her to place God at the center of her life and marriage.

Through her testimony, Bri-Anne shares a powerful story of restoration—how God patiently healed wounds, reshaped priorities, and transformed a relationship built without Christ into a covenant anchored firmly in Him. Her story honors the truth that redemption is often a process, requiring humility, discipleship, and the courage to choose obedience again and again.

● ● ●

The Lord has placed it on her heart to inspire, equip, and empower others to take action that impacts lives. She didn't know at the time how God would bring that mission to fruition, but she chose to follow His lead—and the journey so far has been nothing short of amazing.

Bri-Anne and her husband, Phil, committed their lives fully to Christ together, were baptized, and entered into marriage with a shared desire to honor God. They now serve actively in their church community, leading marriage and family connect groups and walking alongside others who are seeking to understand God's purpose for relationships.

Living in Mililani, Hawai'i, Bri-Anne is passionate about encouraging others to trust God's timing, embrace healing, and believe that what feels broken is never beyond restoration. By contributing her story to *Voices of ALOHA: Daughters of the King*, Bri-Anne hopes readers will be reminded that God restores all things—and that a life surrendered to Him can become a powerful testimony of grace.

Chapter 6

MY BATTLESCAR TESTIMONIES

By: Emari Hunn

I am a survivor of childhood abuse, neglect, and abandonment. I have many battle scars, and I'm proud of them. It wasn't always this way.

Age 0-3 | *Born into Chaos, Raised in Neon Smoke*

1972 May 8th–a little girl was born to a journalist mother and a trailblazing rock and roll bar owner father. The happy family's union was short-lived, and they divorced before I was 3. I lived with my dad while he managed the bar. Soon I learned to serve the bar patrons by changing their ashtrays and delivering their food orders. I claimed the corner booth where I slept. This bar, called The Penthouse, was a popping place in Roppongi, "The City that Never Sleeps", in the heart of Tokyo. It's a city buzzing with bars, clubs, and neon lights, and Dad's bar was the place to be for many foreigners, entertainers, and producers. It looked like a jungle, decorated with sidewalk-find furniture, cultural artifacts, musical instruments, rubber penises, and nude photos covering every inch of the walls and ceiling. Classic rock-n-roll on vinyl was the BGM of choice.

One night I was looking out of the penthouse window; I saw a fire truck passing by, blazing its sirens. Daddy was watching with me for a while. Then suddenly, he ran out of the bar as I watched a ball of fire rise in the distance. Daddy did not come back until dawn, but one worker told me that our apartment had burned down that night. I was told he doused himself with water and ran inside the apartment to save a box of my clothes and a plant. A plant.

That night, on the other side of the city, my estranged mother was feeling uneasy. She turned on her TV to find the news of the fire and instantly knew it was our apartment. She thought I was dead.

We lived in the car for days following the fire. I remember sleeping in the car under the tunnel and peeing by the storm drain. I was enjoying an impromptu camping trip, but what a burden my daddy must have been carrying. When he was talking to the landlord and I found we could not return home, I gave them my best insults I could hurl in defense. Soon Dad and I, along with the

● ● ●

plant and a box of clothes, moved into my aunt's tiny apartment. The only memory I have of that time is that I had seizures, and the house was always dark.

Age 8 | Black Sheep in a Fairytale House

When I was 8, there I was in a single-family home with my dad, his new wife, and a stepsister who was the same age as me. New life with a thrown-together family. My stepsister was the princess and I, a black sheep. Stepmom and the princess would go to her ballet lesson and have dinner out while I scrambled for my dinner. I'd steal money from Dad's coin wallet, and I'd go to a street vendor for dinner. Other days, it was instant hamburger, noodles, or curry, decided by a game of microwave dinner roulette.

One evening, one of the street vendors spoke in shocking detail about how a grown woman looks in her private parts and how a man pleasures a woman. This was my first sexual encounter, a sexual awakening. What a disgusting introduction to what God meant for a beautiful union between a man and a woman. He enticed me to meet him when he closed up his shop at 9pm. Something saved my life that night by telling me not to go. Soon after this, I began experimenting with alcohol. It was easy to get a drink in Japan from any vending machine. I'd sit at my desk in the shared room with my stepsister, obsessing over tape-recording my favorite band on the radio, quietly drinking canned shochu from my bottom drawer. I wonder if my stepmom ever knew.

I was a bully and a tomboy in those years. I had no friends and no adult guidance. My new family had their princess, so they forgot me. So forgotten that one day my skull fracture went unnoticed. I slipped and fell off a mound of construction sand and cracked my head on the drum compactor. When I returned home to tell my dad, he only asked if I was bleeding. I wasn't, so he rolled over and went back to sleep. Later in my teenage years, a doctor asked how many days I had spent in the hospital for the fracture.

I know in my plea for attention; I became a bully. Neighborhood parents told their kids not to associate with me. This is when I experienced the real-life story of "Boy (Girl) Who Cried Wolf" and it pierced my heart. I vividly remember being labeled a liar when I was telling the truth. She didn't believe me, and it stabbed my heart. A piece of me broke that day.

Several years later, my instant family sat me down to tell me I'm moving to live with my birth mother. The monster my dad told me about... someone he said I should fear. Now I'll be living with her. Great.

* * *

Age 13 | *Daily Nightmare on the Train*

When I was 13, my life drastically changed to yet another thrown-together family. A mom I never knew and her husband, new school, new house, new everything. They enrolled me in a school a few towns over, so I began commuting to school. This is when the sexual assault began on the subway. The peak time on the subway in Japan is truly like the movies. They hire "pushers" to shove people into the crammed subways. Once inside, clutching your bag in front of you, it's impossible to move. In those trains, I lived a nightmare of nearly daily sexual assault. Some days I was just groped. Some days, it was rape right on the train. For a time, the same man who followed me daily, even when I changed train cars, targeted me. He would whisper, "Get off at the next station".

I don't know how I kept on living, telling no one. I devoted my life to basketball, and it consumed my life. No one knew about the abuse.

Age 15 | *Abandoned in Paradise*

Do you want to live in Hawaii? That's what my mom asked when I was nearly 15. She said, "It's a beautiful place, and you'd love

● ● ●

it." She brought me to check it out, and before I knew it, I was moving to Hawaii. I bid farewell to basketball, my friends, and my broken family. Leaving everything I knew, I left for a new life in a new country... where I had no one again. I didn't even speak the language.

My mom bought a big house in Kalama Valley and enrolled me at Hawaiian Mission Academy to learn English. Everything seemed to be ready... then she said, "I can't run a business from here... I'm going back." My mother, my lifeline, left me here. Alone in paradise. I had no one. No family, no friends. This was before the internet... heck, it was before the age of the computer! Snail mail took over a month to hear from my friends. International calls cost a ton, so I had to watch when I called Japan and keep it short. To go to school in town, it took me 1.5 hours on two bus lines. I remember my step-aunt giving me a quarter and showing me where the bus stop was. Few memories remain of these devastatingly disappointing days of my life. I was in survival mode, trying to make it day by day, catching a bus to and from school and home.

In my sophomore year, I met a boy who was kind to me and also got to know his incredibly loving family. They ate together, attended church together, served together, and worshipped

• • •

together. I've never seen that kind of togetherness and love, and found that Jesus was at the center of it all. His family showed me a kind of love I've never experienced. They introduced me to Jesus, and I got baptized at 16.

One night, suddenly I woke up as I felt someone touching my private parts. Sensing someone in my room, I squinted to see who it was, and I saw my stepfather's deranged face hovering over me, holding his breath. Fear took over me, but I didn't move. I pretended I was still sleeping; I saw him run out of my bedroom as I turned over.

I ran away that night, and when I frantically tried reaching my mother, I found she was out of the country. Once I got a hold of her, she eventually flew over. Her solution, though, was to get me an apartment. I was only 17 years old. There were more incidents over the following years that fueled my drive to get far away from them.

Age 18-23 | *Lost and Running Wild*

As I promised myself, I ran away to college in Northern CA for my freshman year. My parents never once came to visit me there.

No one sent me a care package. I continued searching for love, but all I found was an absurd amount of alcohol and unwanted sexual advances. My life was a life of self-sabotage in every way possible. One night at a party, my stepcousin's friend raped me while the crowd was at the door watching, hooting and hollering as I endured the horror of the most humiliating day of my life.

The shame of what happened only fueled my anger, and the only way I knew how to cope was to treat myself as unlovable garbage. As I continued trying to run away from my pain, eventually it turned into living by bulldozing through life. I wanted to be in control. I didn't need anyone. It was me against the world.

Married at 23—Divorced by 26 | I Thought It Would Save Me

I fantasized about a perfect marriage, and I thought I found it at 23. With little understanding of love and partnership, it came to an inevitable end quickly. The day I received a call from the "other woman" felt like a bucket of ice water dumped over me. We were not mature enough to survive it. The humiliation of another failure in my life brought me to my absolute lowest, and I tried to kill myself. I didn't know God yet, but looking back, it was God who saved me from my noose.

Remarried at 36 | Meeting My Match–Healing Begins

Years later, I met my match. A boy who's just as broken as me. The one who understands despair, loneliness, and worthlessness. Together we started walking towards healing without even realizing God was leading us. He had a plan for us.

After a few moves by the army, we settled in Albuquerque, NM. This is where I met God. He told me to go to The Wounded Heart, a class for adult victims of childhood sexual abuse. He literally spoke into my heart that night, commanding me to go to the class. I experienced conviction for the first time. Reluctantly I went. There, I learned that I have Jesus on my side. Though I was "a born-again Christian", I never learned that I could have a personal relationship with God. But here in the classroom's safety, I learned for the first time that God is always with me, guiding me, protecting me, and helping me up every time I fall.

Joshua 1:9 (NLT)

"This is my command—be strong and courageous! Do not be afraid or discouraged. For the Lord your God is with you wherever you go."

I thought I was strong, but for the first time in my life, I realized it's okay not to be tough because I am strong in Him. In my brokenness, God is strong.

The thick walls I had built finally started crumbling. God began revealing who He made me to be. As I began my healing journey, I made battle buddies, lifelong friendships, and grew together further by co-leading the class.

The Devil Fought Hard–But God Won

I also learned that the devil attacks even more when you're growing in Christ. Boy, were we attacked! My devil-defying moment arrived when they removed my husband from his position and placed him under investigation. To make matters worse, the authorities arrested him on a military base while our toddler daughter sat in the back seat. Driving to rescue my daughter, I yelled, "I rebuke you, devil! This is not God's plan. Get away

• • •

from our family!" The following 18 months were agonizing, but the meaning of James 1:12 came alive through this season.

Overcoming Obstacles: From Ashes to Beauty

After this season of trials, when we finally saw the light at the end of the tunnel, it was so bright and beautiful. While I thought my husband would lose his career and we'd be homeless, God was preparing a beautiful new beginning. Little did we know the blessings would flow in due season. We bought a house in record time. My husband used his forced free time to get a college degree. Investigation closed, and it was only a slap on his wrist. After this ordeal, he could retire from the Army as a 1st Seargeant with 100% disability. God truly rewards the faithful!

James 1:12 (NLT)

"God blesses those who patiently endure testing and temptation. Afterward they will receive the crown of life that God has promised to those who love him."

Even after this realization, life was not always rosy. Marriage was hard; my husband went through trials figuring out life after the military. Gambling, infidelity, alcohol addiction, and explosive fights plagued us, but one thing was true. God is good all the time. I knew in my soul that He uses everything for good, and faith kept me moving. I focused on my healing, though it was an agonizing process. Having flashbacks and re-living those painful moments brought anxiety and panic attacks. I constantly dreamt of my childhood home where my dad and stepfamily lived. Those were the years I lived in isolation, loneliness, worthlessness, and feeling unlovable. I survived this season because He blessed me with my battle buddies, my Godly council.

From this experience, I truly understood how good God is. God does not waste a single tear. He uses even the most traumatic events in your life and turns them into something beautiful. As I overcame each obstacle in my life, I see now that it was God pulling me up, protecting me, helping me to where I am today. If someone had told me a decade ago that I'd be helping others with their healing journey, I would have laughed. But He did. God uses my experience to bless others with the gift of healing while He continues to heal me. Now I'm committed to serve Him wherever He sends me. He gives me so much joy! I will do what God tells me. God even told me to quit my job once, and I obeyed. The reward: abundant blessings with the best career of my life!

God, I believe. I believe that you have the best plans for me, and you were always there for me. I give my life of service to you to honor you. Thank you for my life.

Your blessed daughter,

Emari.

ALOHA INTEGRATION ~

When Survival Became Strength

If this story felt heavy, pause here.

Do not rush past what your heart or body may be holding.
Some stories awaken memories we thought we had buried. Others stir emotions we never had words for. If you felt unsettled, tender, or deeply quiet while reading—nothing is wrong with you.

Your response is a sign of humanity, not weakness.

This story speaks to endurance—the kind forged not in one moment, but over years. It tells the truth about what prolonged trauma can do to a person, and it honors the courage it takes to keep going when escape is not simple and healing is not immediate.

If you recognized yourself here, hear this clearly:

What happened to you was real. And it was not your fault.

As you reflect, notice how ALOHA carried this journey—sometimes invisibly, sometimes fiercely:

• • •

Overcoming Obstacles

Some obstacles are not single events; they are environments. Survival in these spaces required strength you did not choose—but God saw every moment you endured. Where have you underestimated the resilience it took just to remain alive?

Acute Awareness

Awareness developed through trauma can feel like a burden. Yet God can redeem even this—transforming vigilance into wisdom, and discernment into protection. Where might He be inviting you to release fear while keeping truth?

Health & Healing

Healing from deep trauma is not linear, and it is not rushed by God. Restoration happens layer by layer, often with help. Where might God be inviting you to receive care rather than carry everything alone?

If anger surfaced, let it be named.
If grief rose, let it be honored.
If numbness appeared, let it rest.

God does not demand healing on a schedule. He offers presence instead.

● ● ●

Before continuing, hold this prayer close:

God who sees what others missed,

Thank You for staying when I had no escape.

Hold the parts of me that learned to survive too early.

Restore what was taken, soften what hardened,

and help me trust that I am safe now.

Amen.

About the Author: Emari Hunn is a woman of courage whose life story reflects endurance, truth-telling, and the quiet strength required to survive prolonged hardship. Through her testimony, Emari shares a deeply personal journey marked by trauma, resilience, and the long, sacred work of reclaiming identity and voice.

Her story honors the reality that survival itself can be an act of bravery, and that healing often unfolds slowly—layer by layer, truth by truth. Emari writes with honesty and depth, offering readers permission to acknowledge pain without shame and to recognize strength they may not yet see in themselves.

Emari is married to her husband, John, and together they are raising their beautiful daughter in Pearl City, Hawai'i. Family and faith anchor her life, grounding her journey in love, hope, and the belief that restoration is possible even after the hardest seasons.

She is also an incredible servant to her community on O'ahu and faithfully serves within her church family at Inspire Church, reflecting her heart for compassion, generosity, and Christ-centered leadership.

Rooted in the truth that what is brought into the light can no longer hold power in the dark, Emari's testimony serves as a reminder that endurance is not weakness and that awareness—though forged through difficulty—can become wisdom and protection.

By contributing her story to *Voices of ALOHA: Daughters of the King*, Emari hopes readers who have endured silent battles will feel seen, believed, and reminded that what they survived does not define them—but it does testify to their strength.

Chapter 7

THE DAY THAT COULD HAVE BEEN MY LAST

By Mary Huhnholz

"I will love Thee, O Lord, my strength.
The Lord is my Rock and my Fortress, and my Deliverer;
My God, my strength, in whom I will trust;
my Buckler, and the Horn of my Salvation, and my High
Tower."
Psalm 18:1–2

A LITTLE ABOUT ME

My name is Mary Huhnholz, and I was born and raised in Portland, Oregon. My journey has been full of challenges, but through every hardship I have learned that God is faithful.

Growing up, life wasn't easy. I faced things that no child should, and I carried the pain of it into adulthood. I learned to hide my hurt behind a smile and to survive by being strong. But strength without healing only takes you so far. It wasn't until my life

• • •

completely fell apart that I began to truly understand what God's grace meant.

Through the years, I've battled depression, fear, and pain that tried to destroy me. I've been to the lowest of lows: mentally, emotionally, and physically. But even in those dark places, God never let go of me. He stayed with me through every tear, every panic attack, and every sleepless night.

Today, I'm alive because of His mercy. I have a story to tell, a testimony that shows no matter what we've been through, there is always hope in Jesus. My prayer is that through my words, someone will feel less alone and remember that God can restore what feels broken beyond repair.

I share my testimony not to relive the pain but to glorify the One who saved me from it. Hope is real. Healing is possible. And faith carries us from surviving to truly living again.

CHAPTER I - THE DAY THAT COULD HAVE BEEN MY LAST

August 8, 1985, was the day I died; and the first time I heard the Almighty God's voice. It was a warm day, and I was getting ready to go to work with my mother. She was coming to pick me up. We were cleaning offices at Hewlett-Packard and G.I. Joe's corporate buildings.

That morning, I had a terrible argument with my boyfriend. I told him I wanted to quit doing drugs, but he wasn't ready to stop. I felt trapped; stuck in a corner with no way out and no one to help. I was frustrated, heartbroken, and deeply depressed.

After he left for work, I was home alone. I took a shower, crying the whole time. When I went back to my room, I saw the gun under the bed. I picked it up. The safety was still on. I pointed it toward my stomach, feeling pain and shame, just wanting the hurt to stop. I pulled the trigger. It shot me.

My body went into shock. I was soaking wet and had no feeling from the waist down. "Mom!" I screamed. "Mom!" I needed something wet and cold to put over my face.

Realizing my legs didn't work, I slid off the bed and fell to the floor. I had to lift my legs and place them behind me, then crawled on my stomach, pulling myself forward by gripping the shag carpet. I made my way down the hallway toward a basket where a wet towel from my shower was. I grabbed it; it was still damp and cold; I put it over my face.

• • •

That was when I began praying. "God, please forgive me. Oh Jesus, I don't want to die. I just wanted help from all this pain in my life." I cried, "God, what should I do?" Just then, I heard a comforting voice say, "You need to slow your breathing. I forgive you."

Then God said, "I'm here. I'm with you. I won't leave you." I started feeling very sleepy. I didn't know the extent of the damage. The bullet had torn through my major artery, the aorta that leads to the heart. After that, it bounced around, taking an enormous chunk out of my liver, tearing through part of my stomach, and lodging in my spine.

Just then, my mother showed up and found me. She called for an ambulance. By the time they arrived, I had lost a lot of blood.

I remember being awake when I reached the hospital; they rushed me straight into the operating room. I opened my eyes to bright lights and heard the doctors say, "No, we can't give her anything to put her under because of the blood loss. She may not wake up." Then, suddenly, it felt like a house had dropped onto my chest.

I passed out and saw myself above, looking down at my family and two pastors. I could hear what they were thinking and saying. A doctor came in and said, "Sorry, she's gone. Flatlined." I

• • •

shouted, "I'm right here!" Everyone began praying. Minutes later, the doctor returned and said, "I don't know what you're doing, but keep it up! She's back!"

He said I might never walk again and could have brain damage. I felt a powerful pull and was back in my body. I heard the Lord say, "You must stay here. It's not your time."

CHAPTER II – DEPRESSION, ANXIETY, PANIC ATTACKS, AND DRUGS

After that day, I spent a long time in the hospital, months of pain and recovery. I didn't realize how long it would take to heal, both inside and out.

While I was in the hospital, they administered morphine for pain and prescribed Oxycodone and Vicodin upon my discharge.

Then I started having panic attacks. I didn't even know what they were back then. Each one felt as if I were dying all over again. My heart would race, my chest would tighten, cold sweats would come over me; I ended up in the ER more than once. I was terrified. I thought God was punishing me.

• • •

The doctor said it was anxiety. I didn't understand. I kept saying, "No, something is really wrong with me." But they were right. It was anxiety, depression, and trauma; all mixed together.

At that time, I didn't tell anyone how I felt. I thought people would think I was crazy, so I kept it all inside. Drugs numbed me for a while, but they didn't heal me. In fact, they made the panic attacks worse.

I began hearing voices whispering, "You're worthless. You'll never get better. You're a failure." It scared me. Deep down, I knew that wasn't God's voice.

I prayed and cried, asking God to help me and take those thoughts away. Sometimes peace would come for a little while, then the fear would return.

The panic attacks would start again: heart pounding, hands shaking, short of breath. I truly thought I was going crazy.

Then one night I heard a different voice; soft but strong, say, "Trust Me." I knew it was God. I broke down and wept.

From that moment on, I prayed every morning and every night. Sometimes I didn't have words, only tears, but He understood.

• • •

Slowly, the panic attacks lessened. The voices grew quiet. My faith grew stronger. I learned God had saved me for a reason. He was teaching me to rely on Him, not on drugs or the people around me. Healing took a long time, but now I see that He never left me, not even in my darkest days.

CHAPTER III – HEALTH AND HEALING – I OWE IT ALL TO THE LORD

It wasn't easy after everything I went through. The doctors told me I'd never walk again, but I refused to believe that. I told them, "God is not done with me."

Therapy was painful. I cried a lot but kept pushing myself. Every tiny movement felt like a victory. When I finally stood up for the first time, I thanked God out loud.

The nurse started crying with me and said, "You weren't supposed to be able to do that." I answered, "It wasn't me; it was God."

My faith kept me going even when the pain was bad and progress was slow. Some days I wanted to give up, but the Lord kept telling me, "Keep going." Every day I thanked Him for another chance to walk, to breathe, to live.

● ● ●

It's been years now since the day I was shot. I still have pain, but I'm alive. I can walk. I can laugh. I can love.

People sometimes ask why I believe so deeply. I tell them, "Because I met God."

He was with me when I should have died, when I couldn't walk, and He is still with me today.

If you're reading this and feel you can't go on, remember this: God is real, He is love, and He has a plan for you too. I am a living miracle, and I owe it all to the Lord.

CHAPTER IV – THE END OF THIS PART OF MY LIFE

I thank God every day that I'm still here. He gave me another chance when I didn't think I deserved one. My life isn't perfect. I still have hard days. But every morning, I wake up and say, "Thank You, Lord."

I try to share my story, so others know God still works miracles—because I am one.

If you're struggling, please don't give up. God hasn't forgotten you. He loves you, and He will never leave you.

I've learned that forgiveness sets you free. I forgave my ex-husband, I forgave myself, and I forgave everyone who hurt me. Carrying hate only hurts you, not them, so I let it go.

Now I live my life in peace, knowing exactly who I belong to, Jesus Christ.

One day, I will see Him face to face. Until then, I'll keep walking with Him and tell people what He has done for me.

To anyone reading this, I pray you find hope in my story. God can turn even the darkest night into a new morning.

Thank you for reading my testimony. May God bless you and give you strength to keep going.

The End of This Part of My Life — Mary Huhnholz

Reprinted with permission in Voices of ALOHA; Daughters of the King Anthology Vol. 1 – A Choir of Hope, published by Blessed To Be A Blessing Worldwide Publishing (2026).

• • •

ALOHA INTEGRATION ~

When Mercy Interrupted the Darkness

If you are still here after reading this story, pause.

Life has a way of convincing us that some moments are final—that one decision, one night, one mistake could define the end. And yet, this story reminds us of a holy truth: God specializes in interruption.

If this testimony stirred fear, gratitude, or a quiet ache in your chest, let that settle softly. You are not meant to carry it alone.

This is a story of mercy that stepped in when hope felt out of reach. Not because everything was resolved—but because God refused to let the darkness have the final word.

If you recognized yourself in this story, hear this gently and clearly:

Your life has value beyond what you can see in your hardest moment.

As you reflect, notice how ALOHA carried this testimony into light:

• • •

Health & Healing

Healing does not always arrive as relief first—it often begins as survival. God's mercy meets us at the threshold between despair and breath. Where have you experienced His care simply by still being here?

Affirmations & Actions

Sometimes the bravest action is choosing to live one more day. Speaking life over yourself may begin quietly, even shakily. What truth might God be asking you to hold onto today?

Acute Awareness

There are moments when clarity comes not through answers, but through presence. Where has God shown Himself faithful—even when understanding came later?

If this story awakened gratitude, let it deepen.

If it stirred grief for moments you wish had turned out differently, release that sorrow into God's hands.

If it reminded you how close hope can be—even when unseen—hold onto that truth.

Before turning the page, rest in this prayer:

God of mercy and life,

Thank You for staying when the night felt endless.

Thank You for breath, for presence, for another chance.

Help me trust that You are not finished with me.

Teach me to live the life You have preserved with purpose and
hope.

Amen.

About the Author: Mary Huhnholz is a woman of faith born and raised in Portland, Oregon, where she still lives today. Her life bears witness to the power of God's mercy and the sacred gift of life preserved. Through her testimony, Mary shares a deeply vulnerable moment when her life could have ended—but by God's grace, did not.

Mary's writing reflects honesty, humility, and profound gratitude for the breath she has been given. She offers readers a reminder that even in moments of despair or finality, God is present, attentive, and able to intervene. Her story points gently to the truth that life itself is a calling, and that being here—still breathing, still hoping—is never accidental.

Rooted in faith and awareness, Mary's testimony honors the reality that healing and purpose can emerge from moments that once felt

• • •

overwhelming or hopeless. She writes not to sensationalize her experience, but to testify to God's nearness and the quiet strength that comes from choosing life.

By contributing her story to *Voices of ALOHA: Daughters of the King*, Mary hopes readers will be reminded of their inherent worth, the value of their lives, and the truth that God is not finished with them—no matter how dark a season may feel.

CARRY THE SONG FORWARD

As you've reached this page, you have not merely *read* a book.

You have listened.

You have sat with stories that required courage to tell and tenderness to receive. You have heard voices rise from silence, faith emerge from fracture, and hope sing even when the night felt long. That kind of listening changes us.

And now, gently, the song turns toward you.

This anthology was never meant to end with the final page. It was meant to awaken something—to remind you that testimony is not reserved for the healed, the polished, or the fearless. It belongs to the willing.

The *Voices of ALOHA* movement was born from obedience and community, and it continues the same way. We believe that when one voice speaks truth, others find the courage to rise. When stories are shared in love, healing multiplies.

• • •

Perhaps as you read, something stirred in you. A memory. A realization. A quiet nudge you couldn't quite name.

If so, consider this your invitation.

Your voice matters. Your story has purpose. And what you have lived; no matter how unfinished it feels, may be the very testimony someone else is praying for.

We will continue to welcome stories. We will continue to gather voices. And we will continue to create space for women to share, to heal, and to leave a legacy of faith and courage.

Your story may belong in the next volume of *Voices of ALOHA*.

Not because it is perfect. But because it is real.

Volume II Begins With You

Before you close this book, take a breath.

You have carried seven stories in your hands.
You have listened to courage.
You have witnessed healing.
You have felt faith rise from places that once held silence.

● ● ●

Now, gently… turn inward.

What stirred in you?

What memory asked to be acknowledged?

What part of your own story felt seen for the first time?

You do not need perfect words.
You only need honesty.

Let this be a quiet beginning.

A Gentle Pause

What part of your story have you kept tucked away?

_____

_____

_____

_____

_____

_____

What season shaped you in ways others may not see?

_____

_____

_____

_____

_____

_____

Where did you survive something, you never thought you would?

_____

_____

_____

_____

_____

_____

What truth has God been whispering to your heart?

_____

_____

_____

_____

_____

If your voice felt safe, what would it say?

_____

_____

_____

_____

_____

• • •

As you step forward from these pages, may you carry what you have received with humility and hope. Speak when God invites you to speak. Listen when He calls you to listen. And trust that no voice offered in faith is ever wasted.

Let this be our benediction:

May you walk in ALOHA—
aligned in action, rooted in love,
strengthened through obstacles,
committed to healing,
and awakened to the truth that your voice has power.

The choir is still growing.

And when you are ready, there is room for your song.

Send your story to: voicesofalohamovement@gmail.com